Eat Like a Local

PARIS

BLOOMSBURY PUBLISHING

LONDON • OXFORD • NEW YORK • NEW DELHI • SYDNEY

Eat	14
Drink	78
Shop	100
Cook	130

Welcome to Paris

Paris isn't for lovers. Paris is for eaters. This city is a gastronomic temple worthy of your time and attention. Yes, you should visit the Eiffel Tower, the museums and Notre Dame, but keep in mind that there is a whole other realm of culture and life beyond the monuments that is begging to be explored. Good food and wine is a hallmark of French living, revered like an ancient relic while simultaneously a simple expectation of day-to-day life.

You'll see it wherever you go, from the rows of pristine, art-like pastries in the shop windows, to the smell of fresh warm baguettes or roasting chickens wafting down the street. By law, every neighbourhood must have an open-air market twice a week, because that's the best way to get the best produce, and good food is a basic right. You can hardly know what to get more excited about – a fresh, buttery croissant with a café crème in the morning or the interplay of wine with your cheese plate at dinner.

As you wander around the various charming neighbourhoods of Paris, keep your eyes open for what the city wants to give you. Maybe it's a glass of wine in a quaint little bar, or a gleaming pastry waving to you through the window. Perhaps you'll make an eating itinerary – a morning market stroll, a visit to a cheese shop in the afternoon and then reservations at a classic French bistro where you can go back in time while eating your duck confit. The city is filled with little charms and surprises if you are open and ready to explore.

Explore the City

1st The arrondissement of Paris fashion magazines, filled with ogle-worthy architecture, monuments, parks and squares. Rue Montorgueil is a joy to wander down, with bustling cafés, cheese shops, restaurants and bakeries galore.

2nd Once home to iconic fresh food market Les Halles. Though the market itself was dismantled in 1971 and the area has since gained a modern shopping mall, some of the historic institutions that fed the local vendors still survive (see Au Pied de Cochon, page 34). Rue Sainte-Anne is known as Little Tokyo and has numerous Japanese restaurants and ramen shops.

3rd/4th (Marais) A must-visit. Once the stomping ground of aristocrats, there are impressive mansions sprinkled throughout the *quartier*. The ancient cobblestone streets lend a specific charm and beauty to an area otherwise occupied by luxury boutiques and hip cafés. Rue des Rosiers marks the heart of Paris's Jewish quarter where exceptional falafel shops abound.

5th/6th (Latin Quarter/St Germain) Left Bank Paris at its finest. The 5th is home to Paris-Sorbonne University (and plenty of students) and the market street rue Mouffetard. The 6th is chic, energetic and filled with famous history-steeped cafés and restaurants. There are plenty of noteworthy bakeries, pastry shops and chocolate boutiques to be found on the narrow, winding medieval streets.

7th A chic area filled with embassies, expats and wealthy French families. Though on the residential side, strolling around is still enjoyable as you clock views of the Eiffel Tower peeking through side streets. Rue Cler, a small, pedestrianised street filled with shops and cafés, is the perfect place to buy a picnic to enjoy in the green Champ de Mars.

8th Paris's high-end district that houses the Champs-Élysées, Arc du Triomphe and plenty of *haute couture* boutiques. High prices and limited choice make this somewhat of a no man's land for eating, so it's advisable to explore this arrondissement in-between mealtimes.

9th (Pigalle) What was once the red light district is now a bustling gentrified area popular with Paris's hipster crowd. Some illicitness remains but you'll mostly find stylish boutiques, trendy cocktail bars and modern restaurants.

10th/11th (République/Bastille/Oberkampf) A popular area for those who flock to hip restaurants run by talented young chefs making stellar food. The area between République, Bastille and Père Lachaise cemetery is filled with restaurants, wine bars, gourmet shops and cocktail bars worth crossing town for.

13th (Chinatown) As well as being a hotspot for great Cantonese and Sichuan cuisine, the *Quartier Asiatique* is equally known for its Vietnamese, Laotian, Cambodian and Thai restaurants.

18th (Montmartre) This postcard-perfect arrondissement is popular for day visits but good food can be scarce, as lots of hungry tourists can lead to lots of rip-offs and subpar food. People come in droves to see its beautiful cobblestone streets and the Sacré-Coeur Basilica.

19th/20th (Belleville) It can be a bit out of the way for the average visitor, and slightly rough around the edges, but Belleville is emerging as the next hotspot for restaurants and coffee shops run by young passionate chefs and artisans. Here you'll find high quality coffee, natural wine bars, restaurants surrounded by street art, authentic Chinese food and some in-the-know brunch spots.

Meet the Locals

Julie Neis

parisfoodaffair.com

A besotted Texan who has lived in Paris for over six years. She writes about where to eat and drink in the city on her blog, Paris Food Affair, described as "a place for the France obsessed and the food obsessed".

Joann Pai

@sliceofpai

A food and travel photographer originally from Vancouver and now based in Paris. She has travelled the world working on brand shoots and editorial assignments for the likes of *Vogue*, *Saveur*, *Condé Nast Traveller* and *The New York Times*.

Adrien

foodinparis.fr

A Parisian who uses his popular website to share his curiosity about the inexhaustible playground of Parisian gastronomy. Food in Paris covers new openings, restaurant reviews, budding trends and industry news.

Maeve Schauerman Decouvelaere

parisuncorked.com

LA native who moved to Paris to study wine at Le Cordon Bleu. She founded the website Paris Uncorked as a convenient way of sharing her Parisian food and wine recommendations and is now Wine Associate at Kermit Lynch Wine Merchant.

Lindsey Tramuta

@lostncheeseland

A Paris-based journalist who has written for international publications such as *The New York Times, Condé Nast Traveller* and *Afar* magazine. Her first book, *The New Paris*, was published in 2017.

Natalia Esteves

secretfoodtours.com

A food enthusiast who was raised in Paris and Portugal and has been working in tourism for the last fifteen years. She has lived in cities across Europe and is now the manager of Secret Food Tours in Paris.

Raphaële Marchal

@enrangdoignons

A food author and journalist who has contributed to publications such as *Fou de Pâtisserie* and *Le Fooding*. She has written several books including her latest, *Simple comme bonjour*, and works on events and videos with chefs throughout Paris.

BREAKFAST

So you wake up, and what's the most important thing to check off your list? The Louvre? The Arc de Triomphe? *Non. Le petit déjeuner.* To start the morning right, head to your neighbourhood *boulangerie* or café. The French typically don't do eggs and bacon, that's for the tourists. And besides, with all that flaky, buttery goodness on offer, who needs anything else?

The traditional French weekday breakfast is typically a simple *Viennoiserie* item such as a croissant, pain au chocolat or brioche. Or, when at a café, you can opt for a *tartine*, which is a long sliver of baguette with butter and jam. *Voilà.*

The weekend is a different story. Paris has caught on to the beauty of brunch, and it is *populaire*. It's even a verb now in French *("bruncher"*, to brunch), and if you're not having *le brunch* on Sunday, you're not doing Sunday right. Eggs, pancakes, bacon, potatoes and avocado toast have made their way onto Parisian menus and into the hearts of the French. You can even find quality cocktail bars getting in on the act and opening for brunch on Sundays.

While most French restaurants and cafés have not completely mastered the glory that brunch can be, they're mostly getting there. There are, however, a few restaurants whose brunch game is very much on point, so it's worth scheduling a trip to one or two into your weekend plans.

See also Angelina (page 96), Les Deux Magots (page 35), PÂTISSERIE (page 20)

① Café Oberkampf

Recommended by Joann Pai, Lindsey Tramuta

"I'd recommend the *shakshuka* (Turkish-style eggs in tomato sauce). They serve delicious breakfast items and, most importantly, great coffee"—*JP*

"They serve excellent coffee, *tartines* with all manner of spreads, and also less traditional breakfast options like Bircher muesli and granola. The owner's second location, Café Mericourt, is a five-minute walk away and keeps the breakfast game strong"—*LT*

3 rue Neuve Popincourt 75011
(see website for other locations)
cafeoberkampf.com • +33 143556010
Closed Wednesday and Thursday • €€€€

② Carette

Recommended by Adrien

"It's an old institution in the very touristy area of Trocadéro. But dare to go inside and you will find yourself among the best pastries and brunch dishes. It's not cheap but it's worth a visit"—*A*

4 place du Trocadéro 75016
carette-paris.fr • +33 147279895
Open 7 days • €€€€

③ Holybelly

Recommended by Julie Neis, Joann Pai

"Two Parisians spent time in Melbourne and brought the best of that breakfast and coffee culture back to Paris. Aside from the beautiful skylight, fresh food and friendly staff, there is one reason you must go there: pancakes with fried eggs, bacon and bourbon butter"—*JN*

"Great for a hearty breakfast with good coffee. Go for the pancakes"—*JP*

5 rue Lucien Sampaix 75010
(see website for other locations)
holybellycafe.com
Open 7 days • €€€€

4 Chez Casimir

Recommended by Maeve Schauerman Decouvelaere

"Thierry Breton's brunch on Saturdays and Sundays is a thing of buffet feast dreams. One of my favourite things about this place is that, to choose your wine, you simply head to the wine cave to peruse the bottles and pick your poison"—*MSD*

6 rue de Belzunce 75010
+33 148782880
Brunch served Saturday and Sunday • €€€€

5 KB Coffee Roasters

Recommended by Raphaële Marchal

"I can't imagine a day without a coffee to start, and they do quite an incredible one. *Tartines*, cakes and fresh juices are very good too"—*RM*

53 avenue Trudaine 75009
kbcafeshop.com • +33 156921241
Open 7 days • €€€€

PÂTISSERIE

While a *boulangerie* typically specialises in making bread, a *pâtisserie* is where you want to head for tip-top pastries. *Viennoiserie* (a subset of pastry that hails from Vienna) is your typical breakfast pastry category, and includes the likes of croissants, pain au chocolat and brioche. These are abundantly enjoyed in the morning, with Parisians relishing in layers of light and fluffy buttery pastry and covering themselves with flakes at every bite.

A quirk of the French legal system means that you can always identify a pure-butter croissant simply by the fact that it is straight. If a croissant is curved, it might be made with margarine or any other fat. If it is straight then it has, by law, been made with butter alone. Given that margarine is cheaper and all noteworthy pastry chefs in Paris pride themselves on the quality of their butter, it is straight croissants that are generally considered superior in this city.

Pâtisseries also offer a bounty of the other type of pastry that must be indulged in: dessert pastries. While walking around Paris on any given day, one passes windows and cases filled with beautiful, tiny pastry cakes. It's going to be so difficult to choose, but you can, and you must.

There is an entire host of classic French dessert pastries, and there are a seemingly infinite number of creative pastries that pastry chefs invent on their own. All you can do is try them all, one by one.

See also Angelina (page 96), Gérard Mulot (page 125), Jacques Genin (page 121), Jean-Paul Hévin (page 120), Mokonuts (page 70), Pierre Hermé (page 128)

⑥ Fou de Pâtisserie

Recommended by Joann Pai, Lindsey Tramuta

"I consider it the all-star pastry shop as it has contributions from some of the best *pâtisseries* in Paris"—*JP*

"I go here to pick up pastries or *Viennoiserie* from a variety of leading pastry chefs – the cheesecake from Jonathon Blot of Acide Pâtisserie, the éclairs from Carl Marletti or the Ispahan croissants by Pierre Hermé which are available on the weekend (and often sell out at Pierre Hermé's own boutiques). It's not only about convenience but the sharp selection I can reliably find on each visit"—*LT*

45 rue Montorgueil 75002
foudepatisserie.fr
Open 7 days • €€€€

⑦ Bontemps

Recommended by Adrien

"A unique *pâtisserie* you have to try"—*A*

It is a delight to visit this shop in the Marais near the Marché des Enfants Rouges, even just to look at the beautiful cakes displayed on antique china. There are a wide variety of pastries topped with chocolate, hazelnut, fruits or creams. The shortbread crust used for the pastries is also sold as *sablé* biscuits.

57 rue de Bretagne 75003
+33 142741068
Closed Monday and Tuesday • €€€€

⑧ La Pâtisserie des Rêves

Recommended by Natalia Esteves, Julie Neis

"My favourite pastry is a *Paris-Brest* (choux pastry ring with praline cream) from La Pâtisserie des Rêves"—*NE*

"It's a beautiful store – modern and pink with glass domes over the picture-perfect pastry cakes. You can order individual pastries to go in pretty boxes. Their *chausson aux pommes* (apple turnover) is the best I've ever had"—*JN*

93 rue du Bac 75007
(see website for other locations)
lapatisseriedesreves.com
Closed Monday • €€€€

⑨ La Petite Rose

Recommended by Adrien

"French pastry made by Japanese girls who also make their own chocolates. I love their *Mont Blanc* (chestnut and whipped cream dessert)"—*A*

11 boulevard de Courcelles 75008
+33 145220727
Closed Wednesday • €€€€

. . . .

⑩ Blé Sucré

Recommended by Maeve Schauerman Decouvelaere

"Come for the legendary croissant and stay for everything else. I cross town for these pastries!"—*MSD*

7 rue Antoine Vollon 75012
+33 143407773
Closed Monday • €€€€

CRÊPES & GALETTES

You must get a crêpe at least once while you're in Paris. Imagine strolling down a cobblestone street with a hot and melty Nutella crêpe. Warm hazelnut-chocolatey goodness oozes out as you stare at whichever beautiful thing you're passing. This is the stuff of French dreams – simultaneous sights, smells and tastes. This is the crêpe.

The French don't do a lot of "on-the-go" foods because dining is considered a sacred ritual to be observed with reverence. Normally people will look at you like you're a monster if you eat so much as a banana out in public, but the crêpe succeeds in defying such unspoken rules. So take advantage.

Crêpes come in two forms: a buckwheat flour crêpe (the original, aka *galette*) or a white flour crêpe (that's what you want your Nutella in).

In Brittany (birthplace of the crêpe and champions of butter), locals drink cider out of bowls (yes, bowls) alongside their *galettes*, and the proper crêpe places in Paris will offer the same. It's worth remembering that there is nothing better than having a fried egg on a savoury crêpe. Nothing. And, if you're going for the savoury option, you'll be better off heading to a good specialist crêpe restaurant (savoury crêpes are delicious, but you don't want a crappy crêpe filled with soggy tinned mushrooms, which is what you might get at a crêpe stand on the street).

That said, a dessert crêpe is lovely even at the humble crêpe stand; you can get those with confidence anywhere. If you do go to a proper crêpe restaurant, be sure to get yourself a crêpe with salted butter caramel (*caramel beurre salé*) for dessert, as Brittany is known for excelling in all three elements.

⑪ Brutus Cidrologue & Crêpophile

Recommended by Maeve Schauerman Decouvelaere

"The crêpes are tasty but the impressive *cidre* list is the real draw here. You can find classics as well as obscure, experimental and eclectic varieties on the menu"—MSD

99 rue des Dames 75017
brutus-paris.com • +33 986534400
Closed Sunday and Monday • €€€€

12 La Crêperie de Josselin

Recommended by Julie Neis

"They have a delicious salted caramel crêpe, and it's a fantastic spot to get your traditional (think ham, cheese, egg) savoury *galette* fix without the long wait"—*JN*

67 rue du Montparnasse 75014
Closed Monday and Tuesday • €€€€

13 Breizh Café

*Recommended by Adrien, Julie Neis,
Joann Pai, Lindsey Tramuta*

"Breizh Café is rightfully famous for
its fresh hot *galettes* and cider, but
there is often a line out the door.
Try to call and get a reservation so
you don't have to wait. They have
exceptionally high quality ingredients
including butter and cheese from
Brittany, and the salted caramel
crêpe for dessert is a must"—*JN*

"Though there are many crêpe stands
in Paris, there's only one sit-down
spot whose pancakes *à la française*
soar above the masses: Breizh Café in
the Marais. It's a veritable institution
with locations in Cancale, Saint-Malo
and Tokyo (the owners are a Franco-
Japanese married couple)"—*LT*

*109 rue Vieille du Temple 75003
(see website for other locations)
breizhcafe.com • +33 142721377
Closed Monday • €€€€*

CLASSIC FRENCH

When you go to a traditional bistro or restaurant, the expectation is that you will order a starter *(entrée)*, main *(plat)* and dessert. The meal will be long and leisurely. Don't rush. Have some wine. Expect it to take the whole evening and enjoy the change of pace. A proper French bistro is unfortunately hard to come by, but the ones with owners that know their stuff can really take you back to another time and remind you why French cooking became such a pillar of gastronomy.

Keep in mind that restaurants and bistros tend to be quite small and often require reservations. If you wait until the last minute and hope to walk up, you will likely be turned away. For the most popular places it's best to call and make a reservation a week or two in advance and to confirm it the day before; that way, you won't be disappointed. The full-on way to have a typical French meal is as follows:

Apéritif
Possibly a glass of Champagne, a *kir* (cassis liqueur with white wine) or a *kir royale* (cassis liqueur with Champagne).

Entrée
Typical options include *escargots*, *foie gras*, *pâté* or salad with lardons.

Plat
Menus often feature *magret de canard* (duck breast that typically comes cooked quite pink or *rosé*); *sole meunière* (pan-fried sole with butter sauce); confit duck leg; *boeuf bourguignon;* or any kind of slow-cooked meat.

Fromage
A cheese plate that can either be had instead of or in addition to dessert.

Dessert

For dessert, you'll have lots of options. The French make eyes roll and mouths go silent with reverence and bliss with their desserts. Favourites include *mousse au chocolat*, *Paris-Brest* (a circular pastry filled with hazelnut cream), *moelleux au chocolat* (chocolate cake with a runny centre) and *tarte tatin* (upside-down apple tart).

Espresso

It is common to end your meal with an espresso to aid digestion. You will almost always hear your server ask *"Un café?"* even if it's a late-night dinner.

Digestif

If you're feeling extra full (or not ready for the night to end), then order a *digestif* such as Poire William (a clear brandy made from pears), Cognac (considered one of the finest spirits made from grapes), Armagnac (a popular brandy from south-west France) or Calvados (apple brandy from Normandy). These high proof liqueurs help with digestion after a heavy meal, while also encouraging the conviviality to live on.

⑭ Au Pied de Cochon

Recommended by Julie Neis

"This place has been around for ever and it's one of the only remaining restaurants in Paris that's open 24 hours a day. They have quite a place in history as they used to serve all the vendors who came in the middle of the night to set up at Les Halles market. Their French onion soup is one of the better ones I've found, and if you're feeling brave (or if you really love pork fat), then order the *pied de cochon*, the namesake deep-fried pig's trotter"—*JN*

6 rue Coquillière 75001
pieddecochon.com • +33 140137700
Open 7 days • €€€€

15 Les Deux Magots

Recommended by Julie Neis

"Les Deux Magots was frequented by writers and artists in its heyday and remains a Paris staple. Grab a table on the terrace to enjoy the views of the beautiful Saint-Germain neighbourhood. In the morning, order a café crème and a *tartine* to spread with luscious Échiré butter. Or, for an afternoon treat, try their impossibly thick and creamy *chocolat chaud*"—JN

6 place Saint-Germain-des-Prés 75006
lesdeuxmagots.fr • +33 145485525
Open 7 days • €€€€

16 Les Arlots

Recommended by Raphaële Marchal

"Absolutely heavenly restaurant – loud, chilled, excellent wine list and such great food, purées, sausage, *millefeuille*… I'm never disappointed. And it's all very decently priced"—RM

136 rue du Faubourg Poissonnière 75010
+33 142829201
Closed Sunday and Monday • €€€€

17 Astier

Recommended by Adrien

"Go for their great meat and for the unforgettable cheese"—A

44 rue Jean-Pierre Timbaud 75011
restaurant-astier.com • +33 143571635
Open 7 days • €€€€

18 Josephine Chez Dumonet

Recommended by Julie Neis

"For a classic French institution, with white tablecloths and all, reserve a table at Josephine Chez Dumonet. Sure, as a more upscale bistro it's a bit on the pricey side, but their *boeuf bourguignon* is the stuff of dreams. Their duck confit is crispy on the outside but fall-off-the-bone tender on the inside, and comes served with a side of potatoes fried in duck fat. Don't miss the desserts, either. (If you want the Grand Marnier soufflé, you'll need to order it at the start of your meal)"—*JN*

117 rue du Cherche-Midi 75006
+33 145485240
Closed Saturday and Sunday • €€€€

19 Juste le Zinc

Recommended by Adrien

"The perfect definition of a classic French bistro"—*A*

A neighbourhood bistro on a quiet street with little tables, hardwood floors and a long zinc bar. It has a sophisticated, constantly changing menu, including classics like *foie gras* and *terrine*, but usually with some sort of interesting twist. Their aim is to have a kitchen with cuisine that is simple and traditional, yet with details that aim to surprise.

25 rue de Turin 75008
justelezinc.fr • +33 185152430
Closed Sunday • €€€€

20 Bistrot Paul Bert

Recommended by Julie Neis, Joann Pai

"An excellent choice, especially for dinner when it's usually bustling. They have *sole meunière*, a killer *steak au poivre* and an excellent selection of classic desserts. It has the typical French ambience and atmosphere along with friendly staff who will translate the chalkboard menu for you"—*JN*

"A classic bistro with consistently great food"—*JP*

18 rue Paul Bert 75011
+33 143722401
Closed Sunday and Monday • €€€€

㉑ Chez La Vieille

Recommended by Maeve Schauerman Decouvelaere, Lindsey Tramuta

"Chef Daniel Rose delivers a modern take on classic French dishes made with impeccable produce. If it's on the menu, order the *rognons de lapin* – rabbit kidneys served on sauce-drenched toast – a perfect French dish!"—*MSD*

1 rue Bailleul 75001
chezlavieille.fr • +33 142601578
Closed Sunday and Monday • €€€€

STEAK

Steak frites is known to be a classic dish, found in most restaurants, but the tough, thin cut typically used is neither the best nor the most exciting. If you want good steak, you're better off going to a place that specialises in it.

The French classify their steak differently to other countries, so here are some approximate equivalents that you might find on a menu in a steak restaurant:

Entrecôte Boneless rib eye
Côte de boeuf Bone-in rib eye (big enough for two)
Filet Fillet / Tenderloin
Faux-filet Sirloin
Contre filet Strip steak / Sirloin
Bavette Flank steak
Onglet Hanger steak
Tartare de boeuf Seasoned minced beef, served raw

Your options for how to get it cooked are as follows (keeping in mind that the French like it on the rare side, and they see overcooking beef as a huge *non-non*):

Bleu Blue (a quick sear and still cool in the middle)
Saignant Rare (deep red)
A point Medium-rare to medium (red to pink)
Bien Cuit Well done (why bother?)

You sometimes can't beat a beautifully seared steak, accompanied by an equally beautiful bottle of French red. Looking for an atmospheric, upscale restaurant with bow-tied staff and a well-heeled clientele? Paris definitely has that. Or would you prefer a casual, fun, bustling spot? Paris has that, too. So choose your mood, and go after the *steak frites* of your dreams. Just don't forget the wine.

22 Atelier Vivanda

Recommended by Julie Neis

"Located near the Arc de Triomphe, Atelier Vivanda is a meat and potatoes concept in a modern bistro atmosphere. The starters are always changing, but your options may include risotto, soup, salad or *terrine*. You then choose which meat you'd like as your main and how you would like your accompanying potatoes cooked. At 39€ for three courses, it's a great deal"—*JN*

20 rue du Cherche-Midi 75006
(see website for other locations)
ateliervivanda.com • +33 142714807
Closed Sunday and Monday • €€€€

㉓ Les Parigots

Recommended by Natalia Esteves

"Best meat in my district!"—*NE*

Les Parigots has that old-world French bistro atmosphere that makes you feel like you're part of a never-ending continuum of French tradition. Pull up a chequered bistro chair and dive into some solid food. You'll also find fair pricing with most main courses costing 15–20€.

5 rue du Château d'Eau 75010
lesparigots.fr • +33 185152699
Open 7 days • €€€€

LES PARIGOTS ——— BAR

㉔ La Bourse et La Vie

Recommended by Lindsey Tramuta

"They do an excellent *steak frites* (reviving this humble classic and reminding diners just how good it can be). The *frites* are the right mix of salty and crispy and the chef sources the best meat available for the steak – it makes all the difference"—*LT*

12 rue Vivienne 75002
labourselavie.com • +33 142600883
Closed Saturday and Sunday • €€€€

25 Clover Grill

Recommended by Julie Neis

"Inside you'll find a refined interior with globe lamps, tiled floor, marble tables and beautiful flowered wallpaper reminiscent of the old French style. On the menu (and on display in the meat fridge) you'll find quality steaks from all over the world, waiting to be cooked over the flame grill. You can order à la carte or go for the 69€ *prix fixe*. It can be pricey at dinner, so if you want the experience without the price tag, go for one of their lunch specials"—*JN*

6 rue Bailleul 75001
clover-grill.com • +33 140415959
Open 7 days • €€€€

26 Brutos

Recommended by Julie Neis

"Brutos is run by a French-Brazilian duo and beloved by the natural wine loving community. The standout item, when they offer it, is the *côte de boeuf* – at 90€, it serves 2–3 people and is enormous. The last time I went, the steak was Aberdeen Angus, served with *chimichurri* and toasted cassava flour, salad and *frites*. The starters and other dishes are delicious as well, and they change the menu often according to what's seasonal and fresh"—*JN*

5 rue du Général Renault 75011
+33 148069897
Closed Monday and Tuesday • €€€€

27 Le Relais de l'Entrecôte

Recommended by Joann Pai

"I like going here for *steak frites;* their anchovy butter is to die for".—*JP*

An institution famous for its steak, crispy *frites* and secret-recipe green sauce. There's no menu because steak is your only option. The queue to get in can be notoriously long, so get there just before they open or after the main rush (around 9.30pm). It's a pretty good deal at 40€ for three courses and wine.

15 rue Marbeuf 75008
(see website for other locations)
relaisentrecote.fr • +33 149520717
Open 7 days • €€€€

MODERN FRENCH

If classic French food is rich and heavy, then modern French food is light and fresh. Many chefs employing this style of cooking have a rigorous – if not obsessive – focus on the quality of produce they use, with the principle aim of really elevating the ingredients. They care about where the produce comes from, who's providing it and the farming techniques used. As such, dishes are usually based on what's in season and menus often evolve according to the time of year. In spring, you might see peas and asparagus, and in winter it's likely to be root vegetables such as beetroots and parsnips. And sauces are there purely to bring out the flavour of the produce, not cover or mask.

Part of the fun of modern French food is that flavour combinations are often unique and surprising, and many restaurants go so far as to change their menu daily. The atmosphere is typically laid back and makes for an excellent, yet unfussy, weeknight meal. Some spaces are purposefully designed to feel stripped back and rustic, with exposed walls and bare tile floors, almost as a physical reflection of the pared-back menu ethos.

This style of restaurant has become so popular in the past ten years that some of the most exciting restaurants now fall under this classification of *bistronomy* or *neo-bistro*. It's gastronomy that is accessible – not only in price, but in its relaxed, approachable bistro atmosphere. Chefs have stopped caring about impressing food critics and restaurant guides, and instead are cooking in a way that allows more freedom for experimentation. What results is a style of cooking that is delightful, unexpected and often playful. In Paris, particularly, it's a joy to put your trust in the capability and creativity of a modern French chef.

See also Frenchie Bar à Vins (page 67)

28 Ellsworth

Recommended by Adrien

"A nice option in a pleasant area, close to the Louvre and the Palais Royal" —*A*

Ellsworth is the more casual sister restaurant of Verjus (page 64) and is run by two Americans who got their start by running a wildly popular supper club in their Paris apartment. They have a constantly changing menu of around nine small plates and three desserts. You might find chilli lime ceviche, buttermilk fried chicken, duck meatballs or scallops with kale and cauliflower.

34 rue de Richelieu 75001
ellsworthparis.com • +33 142605966
Open 7 days • €€€€

29 52 Faubourg Saint-Denis

Recommended by Julie Neis, Joann Pai

"The bare concrete walls give an industrial feel to this relaxed, friendly, hip spot on Faubourg Saint-Denis. The cooking is reminiscent of French home-style with a modern twist. You might see duck breast with crispy skin and a fresh medley of vegetables, ravioli with mushrooms, or a deconstructed coq au vin. The prices are really reasonable, and the atmosphere is fun and buzzing"—*JN*

"Offers a creative twist on traditional French cuisine"—*JP*

52 rue du Faubourg Saint-Denis 75010
faubourgstdenis.com • +33 147700686
Open 7 days • €€€€

30 Dersou

Recommended by Julie Neis

"A unique concept restaurant that serves a multi-course tasting menu with cocktail pairings. The food is excellent – contemporary French with Asian influences – and your only choice is how many courses to get. The prices start at 95€ for five courses, but they also have no-reservation Saturday lunch and Sunday brunch menus at a much lower price. It's nice to sit at the bar and get a view of the chefs. If you'd rather a seated table, request it in advance"—*JN*

21 rue Saint Nicolas 75012
dersouparis.com • +33 970385286
Closed Monday • €€€€

31 Septime

Recommended by Julie Neis

"Septime has been one of the hardest restaurants to get into for the past few years, and with good reason. This Michelin-starred restaurant has a rustic and chic interior, friendly service and the outstanding no-choice tasting menu is always changing according to what's in season. They open reservations three weeks in advance. The seven-course dinner menu is 80€, and the four-course lunch menu (which is often easier to get a reservation for) is 42€"—*JN*

80 rue de Charonne 75011
septime-charonne.fr • +33 143673829
Open Monday to Friday • €€€€

32 Le Servan

Recommended by Julie Neis

"This natural wine bistro is fun, energetic and usually bursting at the seams at dinner. The two sisters who run Le Servan incorporate influences from outside of France into their market-driven cooking, and they come up with unique combinations that are beautifully prepared. The menu is always evolving, but you might find barbecued octopus, crispy pork wonton raviolis with tomato water bouillon, raw langoustines with chanterelle mushrooms and caviar, or quail with a spicy shiso celery remoulade. I suggest sharing everything"—*JN*

32 rue Saint Maur 75011
leservan.com • +33 155285182
Open Monday to Friday • €€€€

㉝ Tannat

Recommended by Joann Pai, Lindsey Tramuta

"Doing the classics with better ingredients and more care"—*LT*

An affordable and trendy neo-bistro located in the equally trendy 11th.
The co-owners both worked as chefs at an elegant 5-star Paris hotel and the
kitchen produces modern cuisine using fresh ingredients and seasonal cooking.
Dishes are often Asian-influenced, such as poached fish served in a Thai broth.
You'll find good portions, friendly staff and food that is artistically plated with
colour and flair.

119 avenue Parmentier 75011
+33 953863861
Closed Saturday and Sunday • €€€€

STREET FOOD

Dining is a sacred ritual in France, and they really still live in a way that prioritises a proper sit-down meal over food on the go. Because of that, it can be hard to find any good street food in Paris, which can be frustrating if you need something quick and easy for lunch. You'll have to be savvy, and while sit-down meals are certainly worth your time, it's understandable that every now and then you might need something quick. Your main options are typically a crêpe (page 26), a Turkish kebab or a pizza.

But little by little, Paris is also starting to gain a few food trucks from young, creative entrepreneurs who can be found via social media at weekly markets or along the Berges de Seine (page 59). One other option that can be relied upon and found throughout Paris is the bakery sandwich – the quality is exceptional, even at the most humble of *boulangeries*, as they are made every morning on deliciously fresh French baguettes.

Having said that, keep your eyes open and you might find some weird, wonderful and unexpected options. There is a guy named Alain who makes crêpes and sandwiches in the Marché des Enfants Rouges (page 101) that people are willing to queue for. You'll see the same thing with falafels in the Marais (Paris's historic Jewish quarter) where queues go down the street. It goes to show that a well-made sandwich, falafel or giant gourmet crêpe from a little stand can give just as memorable a foodie experience right there on the streets of Paris.

③④ L'As du Fallafel

Recommended by Joann Pai

"There's a good reason that there is always a line outside. My favourite part about the falafel pita is the marinated aubergine"—*JP*

34 rue des Rosiers 75004
Closed Saturday • €€€€

35 Miznon

Recommended by Adrien, Raphaële Marchal, Joann Pai

"Miznon is living proof that street food can mean quality. Only fresh ingredients are used and they bake their own pita bread. Plus it has a young and funky ambience"—*A*

"Pitas stuffed with houmous, fried eggs, meat or fish and fresh vegetables are served with roasted whole cabbage, cauliflower or beans. So, so good"—*RM*

"I love the cauliflower pitas"—*JP*

22 rue des Écouffes 75004
+33 142748358
Closed Saturday • €€€€

36 Urfa Dürüm

Recommended by Maeve Schauerman Decouvelaere

"It's impossible not to enjoy this Kurdish sandwich served in homemade pita bread, fresh out of the wood-fired pizza oven"—MSD

56 rue du Faubourg Saint-Denis 75010
Closed Sunday • €€€€

· ·

37 Berges de Seine

Recommended by Julie Neis

"If you're going to go for street food in Paris, then it has to be for good reason. The Berges de Seine, a dedicated pedestrian area lining the left bank, has a few restaurants and food trucks on the end closest to Pont Alexandre III. Great for food on the street with a spectacular view"—JN

Quai d'Orsay 75000
Open 7 days • €€€€

SPECIAL OCCASION

Paris is a fantastic place to go for an extravagant meal. If you're planning a special occasion in Paris, you'll need a restaurant that's a step above the rest. There's a myriad of options that can fit the bill, whether you're looking for romantic ambience, a buzzy birthday atmosphere or just that *je ne sais quoi* to help you celebrate being in one of the most beautiful cities in the world.

The city itself is brimming with charm and magic, so much so that you're already at an advantage when venturing out in search of a special and unforgettable evening. Getting a table at the right kind of restaurant, of course, can help elevate your night even further.

Imagine having a swanky evening in Le Clarence (page 62), a luxurious restaurant in an old mansion by the Champs-Élysées. Or perhaps you're after a once in a lifetime 3-Michelin-star experience; L'Arpège (opposite) is just one example of this elite collection of impressive establishments serving unforgettable meals with impeccable service.

You could saunter up a quiet street to dine at a romantic, candlelit restaurant that serves a creative and outstanding tasting menu with carefully selected wine pairings. Or a special night could equally be had at a boisterous and energetic neo-bistro, where outstanding food is served and there is every possibility of making friends with your neighbours, as well as the owners.

Special means something different to each of us. Trust Paris to cater to any and every taste.

See also Compagnie des Vins Surnaturels (page 77)

38 L'Arpège

Recommended by Raphaëlle Marchal

"Highly expensive but there is something so magical about L'Arpège. Not necessarily my favourite interior decoration but experiencing the big menu there is something you'll remember your whole life"—*RM*

84 rue de Varenne 75007
alain-passard.com • +33 147050906
Closed Saturday and Sunday • €€€€

39 L'Ami Jean

Recommended by Maeve Schauerman Decouvelaere

"L'Ami Jean is hands-down my favourite Paris restaurant! It's always a party. Chef Stéphane Jégo cooks up exceptional Basque cuisine and makes sure everyone leaves happy and stuffed to the brim"—*MSD*

27 rue Malar 75007
lamijean.fr • +33 147058689
Closed Sunday and Monday • €€€€

40 Le Gabriel

Recommended by Adrien

"This place will guarantee you a fantastic moment by the chef Jérôme Banctel"—*A*

Le Gabriel is an elegant 2-Michelin-starred restaurant near the Champs-Élysées that often welcomes VIPs and heads of state. Pierre Cardin originally built and designed the building as an upscale boutique hotel in 1986. The cuisine is on the modern side, the service is attentive and the wine list is extensive. Tasting menus start at 180€.

La Réserve Hotel, 42 avenue Gabriel 75008
lareserve-paris.com • +33 158366050
Open 7 days • €€€€

④ Le Clarence

Recommended by Adrien

"With chef Christophe Pelé in the kitchen it will give you the best overview of the romantic side of Paris"—*A*

For a special night of fine dining, try 2-Michelin-starred Le Clarence, which is situated in a restored mansion near the Champs-Élysées. The cuisine focuses on French tradition while revisiting it in modern ways. The wine list is impressive, aiming to showcase some of France's greatest vineyards. Prices for the lunch tasting menu start at 90€ and dinner menus start at €130.

Hôtel Dillon, 31 avenue Franklin D. Roosevelt 75008
le-clarence.paris • +33 182821010
Closed Sunday and Monday • €€€€

42 Verjus

Recommended by Julie Neis

"The dining room at Verjus is intimate and candlelit, with a big walled window overlooking a Paris side street. To me, it's the perfect setting for a romantic dinner for a birthday or anniversary. It's actually an American couple in the kitchen, and their cooking is really fantastic. Their style is upscale contemporary, and it's completely driven by what's fresh at the market. They have a no-choice tasting menu of six to seven courses, all of which are delicious"—*JN*

52, rue de Richelieu 75001
verjusparis.com • +33 142975440
Closed Saturday and Sunday • €€€€

DESSERT & ICE CREAM

It really is a mystery how the French regularly eat butter, croissants, cheese and dessert and still look as great as they do. While they may not eat dessert all the time at home, it is quite normal (and expected) to have dessert when eating out. And with such an incredible selection on offer, how could anyone resist?

You'll notice, wherever you go, that the French are quite reasonable about portion size. Ice cream is usually served as a tiny scoop or two, which is a perfect treat on a warm day. You'll see the famous Berthillon (opposite) sold everywhere on Île St Louis (the tiny picturesque island behind Notre Dame) where it's truly a pleasure to wander with a cone in hand.

For desserts, the kind that you come across will depend largely on the kind of restaurant in which you choose to dine. If the chef is always changing the menu, they'll whip up something new and often seasonal. If you're at a classic French restaurant, then you will have a hard time choosing. Some must-try French desserts include *mousse au chocolat*, *Paris-Brest* (a puffed pastry circle filled with praline cream), *crêpes Suzette* (crêpes flambéed with orange liqueur), *millefeuille* (sheets of puff pastry layered with vanilla pastry cream), *tarte tatin* (upside-down apple tart), soufflé, or *moelleux au chocolat* (a rich, dark chocolate cake with a melting chocolate centre).

See also Angelina (page 96), Jacques Genin (page 121), Pierre Hermé (page 128)

43 Berthillon

Recommended by Julie Neis

"Grab a couple of flavours from Berthillon on Île Saint-Louis and stroll around. It's sold everywhere there"—*JN*

29–31 rue Saint-Louis en l'Île 75004
(see website for stockists)
berthillon.fr • +33 143543161
Closed Monday and Tuesday • €€€€

44 Frenchie Bar à Vins

Recommended by Maeve Schauerman Decouvelaere

"It is no secret that Frenchie Bar à Vins offers high quality food but it can be a challenge to get a table at peak hours. Instead, hold off and head there later in the evening for top-notch desserts! The *pot au chocolat* topped with olive oil and sea salt is exquisite in its simplicity, and the seasonal toppings on the panna cotta are as fresh as can be"—*MSD*

6 rue du Nil 75002
frenchie-restaurant.com • +33 140399619
Open 7 days • €€€€

45 Il Gelato del Marchese

Recommended by Adrien

"An authentic Italian place for ice cream. The pistachio flavour is among the best you can find in Italy, let alone Paris"—*A*

3 rue des Quatre Vents 75006
ilgelatodelmarchese.com • +33 146347563
Open 7 days • €€€€

46 Une Glace à Paris

Recommended by Natalia Esteves, Lindsey Tramuta

"Berthillon (page 67) is an ice cream institution in Paris, but I'm team Une Glace à Paris – a *glacier* co-run by Emmanuel Ryon, a *Meilleur Ouvrier de France*. He always has a handful of smoked vanilla flavours, three different sorts of coffee (including a sorbet) and fruit flavours that taste like you've just bitten into the whole fruit itself"—*LT*

15 rue Sainte-Croix de la Bretonnerie 75004
une-glace-a-paris.fr • +33 149969833
Closed Monday and Tuesday • €€€€

47 Mokonuts

Recommended by Raphaële Marchal

"They're as good a restaurant as they are a pastry shop but, honestly, a piece of pie at Mokonuts is life. Whether apricot, rhubarb or strawberry, they're just the best"
—RM

5 rue saint Bernard 75011
+33 980818285
Closed Saturday and Sunday • €€€€

SMALL PLATES & WINE

Natural wine served alongside small plates of food is a big trend in Paris. It's in these establishments where some of the freshest and most interesting food is currently being made, and where you can eat and drink at the hands of passionate and creative chefs and sommeliers in an atmosphere that is light, fun and energetic.

A real draw is that, instead of choosing the traditional three courses, you can order however many dishes of whatever looks good and get plate after plate. This way, you get to try far more than you ever could at a traditional restaurant. If you go with several people, you could genuinely get everything on the menu and re-order as you please. The chefs at these restaurants are changing their menu all the time, sometimes daily, according to what's fresh and seasonal at the market. Their focus is often on elevating the product and keeping it simple but interesting.

As well as serving excellent food, these kinds of places embody the word *convivial*. They are fun and bustling, the chef is either behind the bar or in the kitchen, and you sit with anticipation waiting for the next plate to come out as you drink your wine. There are interesting wines by the glass – and even more interesting ones by the bottle – and no one is in a rush.

Often the wine list will comprise solely natural wines, which are made with minimal intervention, naturally occurring yeasts and/or minimal use of sulphites or other additives. Natural wines are interesting and different, and range from juicy and super-drinkable to funky and farmy. Just let the sommelier know what you like.

See also APÉRO (page 78), Frenchie Bar à Vins (page 67), Le Mary Celeste (page 88)

48 ## Le Grand Bain

Recommended by Julie Neis

"It's a bit out of the way in Belleville but the menu always has something new, the food is plated simply but beautifully, and the cooking is extremely fresh and seasonal. The space is well designed with low lighting, rustic wood tables, a central bar (which is great for solo diners) and a semi-open kitchen where you can see what's happening behind a big glass window. The menu is presented on a tall blackboard and changes daily. I even enjoy the walk down the little passageway covered with street art. It's a laid-back but energetic spot that's well worth crossing town for. Reservations are a must"—*JN*

14 rue Dénoyez 75020
legrandbainparis.com • +33 983027202
Open 7 days • €€€€

49 ## 116 Pages

Recommended by Adrien

"It's the annexe of a gastronomy restaurant owned by a Japanese chef cooking French cuisine. At 116 they cook octopus, chicken and tuna on the Japanese barbecue (*binchotan*) and serve a huge selection of natural wines"—*A*

2 rue Auguste Vacquerie 75116
116pages.fr • +33 147201045
Closed Saturday and Sunday • €€€€

50 Lucien La Chance

Recommended by Maeve Schauerman Decouvelaere

"Set in an old sweet shop, this natural wine bar offers small plates that change with the seasons. The wine list is always evolving and the guy who runs it loves to talk about what's new and what's tasting well at the moment. A gem!"—*MSD*

8 rue des Dames 75017
lucienlachance.fr
Open 7 days • €€€€

⑤¹ La Cave à Michel

Recommended by Raphaële Marchal, Julie Neis

"Feels like home. It's a small place where you can stand at the bar counter. Wine everywhere, music, and small plates made in front of you. Heaven"—*RM*

"The small, popular natural wine bar is standing room only so go early if you want a less crowded and calmer experience, or go at peak time to squeeze in with others drinking good wine and sharing good food in close quarters"—*JN*

36 rue Saint-Marthe 75010
+33 142459447
Closed Monday and Tuesday • €€€€

52 La Buvette

Recommended by Lindsey Tramuta

"Paris isn't a city that stays up late. However, at most wine bars, like La Buvette in the 11th, quality nibbles are offered right up until closing time. Fresh cheeses, rustic bread, charcuterie, olives and pickled vegetables do the trick"—*LT*

67 rue Saint-Maur 75011
+33 983569411
Closed Monday • €€€€

. . . .

53 Compagnie des Vins Surnaturels

Recommended by Natalia Esteves

"For great wines and snacks. The place is kind of secret because there's no name at the entrance. They have amazing wines and the atmosphere is very romantic"—*NE*

7 rue Lobineau 75006
compagniedesvinssurnaturels.com • +33 954902020
Open 7 days • €€€€

APÉRO

If there was ever a French tradition to engage in while on holiday, it's the social ritual of apéro. Apéro is short for *apéritif* (a pre-dinner drink). The French eat late, 8pm or later, and most restaurants don't even open until 7pm for dinner service (and only the tourists eat at that time).

The purpose of apéro is to have a drink that stimulates your appetite as dinner approaches. Often it's just a good excuse to be social and sometimes, when you have a late dinner reservation, it's the perfect opportunity for a little pre-dinner snack. Drinks are usually served with something small such as peanuts, olives or crisps, but if you're feeling particularly peckish, you should get a charcuterie board and partake in some delicious *saucisson*, *jambon cru*, *terrine*, *rillettes*, or all of the above. (It's worth noting that, while many countries would accept a cheese board as an appetiser, the French have their cheese exclusively after dinner for fear of the richness and creaminess ruining one's appetite. A few slices of cured pork products, on the other hand, will often hit the spot.)

For most people, the typical choice of drink for apéro is Champagne, wine or beer. Some go for a cocktail, while others indulge in a classic aperitif, some examples of which include *kir* (crème de cassis, a sweet blackcurrant liqueur, topped with dry white wine, traditionally Bourgogne Aligoté), *kir royale* (the same thing but with Champagne instead of wine), Pastis (tastes of liquorice and herbs, usually with some added water and ice cubes, popular in the South of France), or Lillet (a fortified wine that can come as red, white or rosé). Go ahead and pick your poison.

See also Causses (page 110), Frenchie Bar à Vins (page 67), SMALL PLATES & WINE (page 72)

54 La Palette

Recommended by Adrien

"La Palette in Saint-Germain is where the young go for an apéro and to mingle with the artists and famous people living in the area. A bottle of wine to share will make everyone happy"—*A*

43 rue de Seine 75006
cafelapaletteparis.com • +33 143266815
Open 7 days • €€€€

55 La Fontaine de Belleville

Recommended by Joann Pai

"Not only is this newly renovated café beautiful, the staff are friendly and
I love the vibe there. It's been my go-to since the day it opened, especially on
Saturday evenings for live jazz!"—*JP*

31–33 rue Juliette Dodu 75010
+33 981755454
Open 7 days • €€€€

56 ## Pratz

Recommended by Maeve Schauerman Decouvelaere

"Pratz is a fantastic *cave à manger* offering a precise selection of natural wines and delicious *épicerie* products including tapenades, burrata, chorizo and, my personal favourite, truffle ham! Wine bottles are priced for takeaway but can be enjoyed *sur place* for a small corkage fee. Thomas curates the wine selection and offers excellent guidance"—*MSD*

59 rue Jean-Baptiste Pigalle 75009
pratz-paris.com • +33 177106703
Closed Monday • €€€€

57 ## La Cave du Paul Bert

Recommended by Raphaële Marchal

Sister restaurant to Bistrot Paul Bert (page 39) that offers delicious market-fresh small plates and an excellent selection of natural wines by the glass and bottle. They do a great job of providing interesting wines made with love by independent winemakers, and you can buy bottles to take home at retail prices. It's mostly standing room only, but if you come early, you can snag one of the few tables. It's a great spot for a casual apéro or for a full evening meal.

16 rue Paul Bert 75011
+33 158535092
Open 7 days • €€€€

58 ## Le Baron Rouge

Recommended by Joann Pai

"This no-nonsense, laid-back wine bar is loved by locals and is a particularly great spot for reasonably priced oysters and wine"—*JP*

1 rue Théophile Roussel 75012
+33 143431432
Open 7 days • €€€€

59 Septime la Cave

Recommended by Raphaële Marchal

"Romantic, small, great bottles and amazing small plates to open your appetite. Love it"—*RM*

3 rue Basfroi 75011
septime-lacave.fr
+33 143671487
Open 7 days • €€€€

COCKTAILS

Being the country of the wine obsessed, it has taken a long time for quality cocktails to make their way to Paris. Fortunately there are now a range of craft cocktail bars to choose from, and the only real dilemma you'll have is whether to get your cocktail before or after dinner. The French do not usually drink cocktails with their meals because strong liquor and other mixers will overpower the subtle flavours found in most French cooking. Wine is of course the drink of choice to have with meals, which means your cocktails will need to be consumed either side.

It was really the Experimental Cocktail Group (see Grand Pigalle, page 86 and Compagnie des Vins Surnaturels, page 77) that championed the craft cocktail movement in Paris, opening three different bars that offered incredibly unique mixed drinks with quality ingredients. They also did a great job of making their places a bit exclusive with a speakeasy vibe. Sometimes you could walk right past the door, knowing you were looking for the place, and think it must have closed down. Yet just behind a no-nonsense unmarked door is a hip bar packed to the brim and serving some of best craft cocktails in town.

Others have followed suit, and now you can find plenty of options for a pre- or post-dinner drink. Most cocktail bars can be found in the 10th or 11th (where most of the best food is, too), with several more located in the 9th around Pigalle.

⑥⓪ La Commune

Recommended by Lindsey Tramuta

"La Commune in Belleville is the second French spirits-focused bar from the
founders and owners of Le Syndicat (page 89). It's fun, relaxed and brings
serious flavour to the cocktail scene"—*LT*

80 boulevard de Belleville 75020
syndicatcocktailclub.com
Open 7 days • €€€€

61 Grand Pigalle

Recommended by Lindsey Tramuta

"At the Grand Pigalle, expect the Experimental Cocktail Group's decade of experience in mixology to shine. (And if you're spending the night, you'll have cocktails in your minibar and can get more delivered to your room!)"—*LT*

29 rue Victor Massé 75009
grandpigalle.com • +33 185731200
Closed Monday • €€€€

62 Le Mary Celeste

Recommended by Raphaële Marchal, Joann Pai

"Paris's cocktail scene has really blossomed in the past few years; my recommendation would be Le Mary Celeste"—*JP*

A cocktail and oyster bar that also has a great selection of small plates. They've created a fun atmosphere with dim lighting and good music. It's ideal for pre-dinner drinks, but you could easily spend the whole evening there. They only take reservations for 6pm to 7pm otherwise it's first come, first served.

1 rue Commines 75003
quixotic-projects.com
Open 7 days • €€€€

63 Lulu White

Recommended by Maeve Schauerman Decouvelaere

"A chic, speakeasy-type bar on an otherwise rather rowdy block, offering expertly crafted cocktails. The playlist is on point and the bartenders are clearly having a good time"—*MSD*

12 rue Frochot 75009
luluwhite.bar • +33 983589332
Closed Sunday • €€€€

· ·

64 Le Syndicat

Recommended by Raphaële Marchal

"I love Le Syndicat, it is so different from anything you know, and the cocktails are fantastic. (And it's ranked among the World's 50 Best cocktail bars)"—*RM*

51 rue du Faubourg Saint-Denis 75010
syndicatcocktailclub.com • +33 666635760
Open 7 days • €€€€

HOT DRINKS

When in Paris, these are your basic coffee options:

Café crème Espresso with milk (similar to a latte)

Café allongé Espresso with hot water (similar to an Americano)

Cappuccino Just what you'd expect

Espresso Also what you'd expect

Noisette An espresso with a bit of hot milk or foam

A *café crème* is the typical breakfast coffee (no one really says *café au lait* any more), and the French don't tend to drink milk-based drinks beyond midday. After lunch it's time for espresso (so forget about the afternoon and evening *café crèmes* and cappuccinos if you want to be culturally savvy). Truthfully, many a Paris café could stand to improve their coffee game. It's actually the Australians who have really brought the culture of excellent coffee to Paris and there are now numerous speciality coffee shops around the city.

The French don't have the kind of tea culture that you see in England, China, Japan or elsewhere, but if you're not into coffee, every café will have some tea options for you. There are quite a few speciality tea stores around Paris (the most widely known is Mariage Frères, found all over the city), and this can make a great gift or souvenir to bring home.

If you're in Paris when the weather is cooler, seek out a rich and creamy *chocolat chaud*. It's thick, velvety and, if you're a chocolate lover, a must-try. This is true decadence, and you may never be able to go back to powdered hot cocoa again.

See also Café Oberkampf (page 15), Les Deux Magots (page 35), Jacques Genin (page 121), Jean-Paul Hévin (page 120), KB Coffee Roasters (page 19)

65 Ten Belles

Recommended by Julie Neis

"There's not much space to hang out, but you can take your coffee to go and sit on the Canal"—*JN*

10 rue de la Grange aux Belles 75010
tenbelles.com • +33 142409078
Open 7 days • €€€€

66 Télescope

Recommended by Maeve Schauerman Decouvelaere

"Both the espresso and *café filtre* at Télescope are meticulously prepared and show distinct flavour profiles. The owls that decorate the café and photogenic blue espresso cups are a plus!"—*MSD*

5 rue Villedo 75001
telescopecafe.com
Closed Sunday • €€€€

67 The Broken Arm

Recommended by Julie Neis

"The café at The Broken Arm is located right in the middle of the Marais, and it's a perfect spot to get a caffeine boost in a pretty setting"—*JN*

12 rue Perrée 75003
the-broken-arm.com • +33 144615360
Closed Sunday and Monday • €€€€

68 Lily of the Valley

Recommended by Lindsey Tramuta

"For tea lovers, Lily of the Valley is a herbaceous tea salon with more varieties than you can count (and they do a wonderful iced tea)"—*LT*

12 rue Dupetit-Thouars 75003
(see website for other locations)
lilyofthevalleyparis.com • +33 157408280
Open 7 days • €€€€

⑥⑨ Boot Café

Recommended by Julie Neis

"Boot Café has an adorable exterior that begs to be photographed. It's so small that you'll likely have to take your coffee to go"—*JN*

19 rue du Pont aux Choux 75003
+33 626411066
Open 7 days • €€€€

⑦⓪ Fragments

Recommended by Adrien

"A coffee shop in Le Marais. In summer they have an ice coffee with soya milk, which is the best in town. And if you are hungry they have pastries and also a very good avocado toast"—*A*

76 rue des Tournelles 75003
Open 7 days • €€€€

71 Coutume Café

Recommended by Julie Neis

"Any coffee lover will love visiting Coutume Café in the 7th, but it's best to go if you want to sit and linger as it's not always quick when they're busy. They have a 24-hour drip/cold extraction brew that some say is life-changing. The device they use looks like a time machine, which certainly makes the experience unique and memorable. The siphon coffee, a fun spectacle to behold, takes you back either to another era or to your school chemistry class. It's a great spot to hang out for a couple of hours and rest your feet or catch up with friends"—*JN*

47 rue de Babylone 75007
coutumecafe.com • +33 145515047
Open 7 days • €€€€

72 Angelina

Recommended by Julie Neis

"If you only go to one spot for hot chocolate in Paris, it has to be Angelina. They are rightfully famous for their *chocolat chaud à l'Africain*, named after the combination of three varieties of African cocoa beans from Niger, Ghana and Ivory Coast. They have several options with varying types of chocolate, but this one is the most renowned. Their hot chocolate is done in the traditional style, which means that it's so rich and decadent that it's basically like sipping on a melted chocolate bar. When it's cold outside, or if you just love chocolate, there can be nothing better"—*JN*

226 rue de Rivoli 75001
(see website for other locations)
angelina-paris.fr • +33 142608200
Open 7 days • €€€€

73 Café de Flore

Recommended by Julie Neis

"Many claim that Café de Flore has one of the best hot chocolates in the city. Sitting on the terrace of this prestigious café gives you that certain awareness of being steeped in a piece of Parisian history – the café dates back to the 1880s and has been a hotspot throughout the decades for famous writers, artists, publishers and philosophers. Your little pot of steaming, velvety-smooth hot chocolate can be ordered with a glass of whipped cream to go along with your people watching. The terrace is heated in the winter, making it a perfect stop on a cold day"—*JN*

172 boulevard Saint-Germain 75006
cafedeflore.fr • +33 145485526
Open 7 days • €€€€

74 Dose Dealer de Café

Recommended by Maeve Schauerman Decouvelaere

"Dose offers two different *chocolat chaud* options – normal and *à l'ancienne*. I like to go for the latter, which is thicker, creamier, more deeply chocolatey and such a treat"—*MSD*

82 place du Dr Félix Lobligeois 75017
(see website for other locations)
dosedealerdecafe.fr
Closed Monday • €€€€

75 La Mosquée Salon de Thé

Recommended by Joann Pai

"For green tea and Moroccan treats. The courtyard is beautiful"—*JP*

There is a charming tea salon within the Grand Mosquée de Paris (founded in 1926), which makes for a calm retreat in the midst of the bustling 5th. Within the walls of the mosque, you'll feel transported to Morocco as you admire the ornate mosaic tiles, arches and blue tiled tables. Sit back and sip hot mint tea with baklava, Turkish delight or North African pastries. The front patio is always busy, so head to the back terrace for a bit of calm.

39 rue Geoffroy Saint Hilaire 75005
+33 143313820
Open 7 days • €€€€

MARKETS

You really know you're in France when you're wandering down a lively Parisian open-air *marché*. It's the epitome of French culture. Each neighbourhood has one at least twice a week and it's incredible to see how much the locals still engage in the tradition. Yes, there are supermarkets that can provide convenience, but here you have access to the freshest produce straight from the supplier.

Since France segments their specialties into individual shops – the butcher, the baker, the cheesemonger, the fishmonger, the pork man, the greengrocer – the market is the best place to go to get all the most delicious items in one place. When you go to a stand, the person working there will pick your fruit or vegetables for you and put them in a bag to weigh. You can let them know, for example, if you want to eat your avocado or melon right now or in three days, and they'll select the best one for you.

You can stumble upon a neighbourhood market while out and about in the city, but there are some extra special ones that are a bit larger and have a greater variety of stands, including some of the best purveyors from around Paris. The Enfants Rouges covered market in the Marais (opposite) is almost as much a food hall as a stop for groceries since it has several restaurants and stands meant for lunch that you can eat at nearby tables (after picking up your flowers and vegetables).

For an indoor food-lover's paradise, you can't beat a trip to La Grande Épicerie (page 102). It's not quite the same as a going to an outdoor market, but the variety of gourmet foods available makes it a notable address.

76 Marché des Enfants Rouges

Recommended by Natalia Esteves, Joann Pai, Lindsey Tramuta

"I love strolling the Marché des Enfants Rouges (the oldest covered market in Paris), which has food stalls featuring cuisines from around the world as well as an organic produce stand, a florist and small restaurants"—*LT*

39 rue de Bretagne 75003
Closed Monday • €€€€

77 La Grande Épicerie de Paris

Recommended by Adrien, Julie Neis, Lindsey Tramuta

"They've got a huge cheese department that I love to visit during my Saturday shopping"—*A*

"The Grande Épicerie gourmet food hall of Le Bon Marché is ripe with food gifts to bring home. You can get Michel Cluizel's single-origin chocolate bars, Christine Ferber jams (they are pricey but people are obsessed with them), every flavour imaginable of Maille mustard jars, a pretty box of French salts, Bretagne cookies, or a jar of salted caramel sauce. They also have beautiful tote bags that you'll probably want to buy for yourself"—*JN*

"A must-visit. Its food stalls make it easy to pick up a ready-made meal but it's also bursting with beautiful produce and artisanal products"—*LT*

38 rue de Sèvres 75007
lagrandeepicerie.com
+33 144398100
Open 7 days • €€€€

78 Marché d'Aligre

Recommended by Raphaële Marchal

"My favourite is Marché d'Aligre, both indoor and outdoor. I could just wander around it forever"—*RM*

A popular choice for Parisians, so much so that it's worth making this your main market visit. Stands line the street, filled with vegetables, fruits, cheeses, roasted chicken, olives, oysters, herbs and more. There is also a flea market in the middle where you might pick up an old treasure.

Place d'Aligre 75012
marchedaligre.free.fr
Closed Monday • €€€€

79 Marché Couvert Batignolles

Recommended by Maeve Schauerman Decouvelaere

"Home to multiple produce stands, a butcher, two fishmongers, a cheese shop, wine cave and more. On the northern rue Brochant side you'll find one of my favourite *boulangeries*, which has the best chocolate chip cookies in Paris, excellent buttery and flaky croissants and fresh rye bread"—*MSD*

96bis rue Lemercier 75017
Closed Monday • €€€€

80 Marché Président Wilson

Recommended by Adrien

"You can find very nice, fresh products in the Marché Président Wilson in the 16th. It's also where some of the city's famous chefs come to buy produce for their restaurants"—*A*

Avenue du Président Wilson 75016
Open Wednesday and Saturday • €€€€

81 Marché Bastille

Recommended by Julie Neis, Joann Pai, Lindsey Tramuta

"The Marché Bastille, also known as the Richard Lenoir, is one of my favourite markets in the city. The atmosphere is lovely, and you can collect a great picnic to eat for lunch somewhere atmospheric like the point of the Île de la Cité. It starts at metro Bastille, and is only on Thursdays and Sundays from 9am until 1pm (though they sometimes start shutting down around noon)"—*JN*

"There are so many outdoor markets but I particularly love the Bastille market which brings together exceptional artisans and farmers twice a week"—*LT*

8 boulevard Richard Lenoir 75011
Open Thursday and Sunday • €€€€

PICNICS

There is nothing better than a picnic on a warm summer evening while staring at some huge beautiful monument. This is a national pastime and Paris hosts a range of gorgeous picnic spots with giant beautiful things to stare at: the Eiffel Tower, Les Invalides, Notre Dame, the bridges on the Seine, Luxembourg Gardens and so on and so on. There is hardly a thing more beautiful or memorable than sitting on the bank of the Seine watching the sun glow fiery shades of orange as it sets behind the Pont des Arts. There you are, alongside the theatregoers, eating your creamy cheese and drinking your wine and wondering why you live anywhere but under a bridge in Paris.

One of your meals deserves to be a picnic, ideally a dinner when you can watch the sunset. Shopping for a picnic is half the fun because the French still segment their artisanal products into small shops that specialise in making that one thing – there's the cheese maker, the bread maker, the chicken roaster, the charcuterie shop, the wine specialist – and each purveyor knows their product in intimate detail and can help with recommendations. An equally enjoyable experience is visiting an open-air market, where you can get everything in one place.

See page 136 for a guide to the perfect gourmet picnic.

See also CHEESE (page 112), MARKETS (page 100)

82 Lenôtre

Recommended by Adrien

"They will offer you the finest picnic"—*A*

Monsieur Lenôtre modernised French pastries in the 1950s by making them lighter and by only ever using the freshest ingredients. His establishment expanded not only into cakes and chocolates, but a whole world of catering. A luxury brand, they offer many gourmet treats in their boutiques, and are deemed one of the pillars of French pastry.

10 rue Saint-Antoine 75004
(see website for other locations)
lenotre.com • +33 153019191
Open 7 days • €€€€

83 Cooperative Latte Cisternino

Recommended by Maeve Schauerman Decouvelaere

"Pick up a couple of Italian cheeses, some speck and *jambon blanc*, a bottle or two of Italian wine and you're all set for that picnic! This Italian *épicerie* also has some of the best fresh pasta in Paris"—*MSD*

46 rue du Faubourg Poissonnière 75010
(search online for other locations)
+33 147703036
Closed Saturday and Sunday • €€€€

84 Kili Kio

Recommended by Raphaële Marchal

"I'd go to Kili Kio for some Greek treats like smoked aubergine caviar, feta and olives"—*RM*

34 rue Notre Dame de Nazareth 75003
kilikio.com • +33 983338824
Closed Sunday • €€€€

85 La Maison Plisson

Recommended by Lindsey Tramuta

"Food emporiums and markets, large and small, are often the best places to procure snacks. La Maison Plisson is located in the north Marais and doubles up as a bakery, gourmet grocer and canteen"—*LT*

93 boulevard Beaumarchais 75003
lamaisonplisson.com
Open 7 days • €€€€

86 Causses

Recommended by Natalia Esteves

This gourmet food store has a good selection of seasonal fruits and vegetables. They also have high quality cheeses, charcuterie, meats, olives, nuts, dried fruit, wines and olive oils. Wandering the aisles itself is fun, but you could really stock up on some things to bring back home or to enjoy for apéro.

55 rue Notre Dame de Lorette 75009 (see website for other locations)
causses.org • +33 153161010
Closed Sunday • €€€€

CHEESE

Cheese. Beautiful, smelly cheese. The French have wooed dairy into all sorts of incredible forms and there is an entire, mind-boggling range starting from the creamy and soft, spreadable cheeses that slather perfectly onto a fresh baguette, to hard, sliceable cheeses with their salty and nutty depth that will have your eyes rolling. Somewhere along that spectrum, you've got tangy goat's cheese and pungent, salty blue cheese. And then some cheeses can admittedly wander into sweaty feet territory, so there's truly something for everyone. And it is completely normal for French families to have a selection of cheeses on hand on any given day to bring out after dinner.

The French typically eat soft cheese on a piece of baguette, hard cheese on its own, and semi-soft cheese either way. Don't expect any crackers (why would you have a cracker when you can have a baguette?) and, when it comes to the rind, the general rule is that you eat it on soft cheeses, but you cut it off hard cheeses.

Brilliantly, there are several cheeses (hard ones in particular) that can come home with you on the plane. You can ask the cheese shop whether they vacuum-seal cheeses, and then throw it in your checked luggage where it will stay cold under the plane. Comté is a great choice for a take-home cheese (so long as your destination allows it).

Cheese shopping is fun and super French, so go squeeze into a tiny shop, wait for an attendant to help you, and then tell them what you're looking for, what you like – mild, strong, hard, soft, blue, goat's– and how much you're after. (But seriously, get the Comté.)

See page 137 for a guide to the perfect cheese board.

See also MARKETS (page 100)

87 Fromagerie Goncourt

Recommended by Lindsey Tramuta

"I always prefer to go to individual cheese shops rather than pick them up at a one-stop shop. My neighbourhood favourite is Fromagerie Goncourt, which is small but brimming with a wide selection of cheeses from regions across France. They also carry one of my favourite honey brands, Hédène, with mono-floral varieties produced with the help of beekeepers across France who use traditional apiary techniques"—*LT*

1 rue Abel Rabaud 75011
+33 143579128
Closed Sunday and Monday • €€€€

88 Taka & Vermo

Recommended by Joann Pai

"A small cheese shop with an amazing selection"—JP

61bis rue du Faubourg Saint-Denis 75010
+33 148248929
Closed Monday • €€€€

89 Le Bel Ordinaire

Recommended by Raphaële Marchal

"They have a nice selection of cheese and are open until midnight, which is always good for a last-minute apéro"—*RM*

54 rue de Paradis 75010
lebelordinaire.com • +33 146274667
Closed Sunday and Monday • €€€€

90 Les Fromages des Batignolles

Recommended by Maeve Schauerman Decouvelaere

"Great selection and helpful staff who often offer samples!" —*MSD*

A neighbourhood *fromagerie* situated in the Batignolles covered market (page 104). If you find yourself near the 17th, they have a large selection of cheeses that should fit your dairy needs. Most cheeses can be cut to the exact size you're looking for, whether you need a little bit for a picnic or a lot for a group (or to bring home). There is also a selection of charcuterie and Italian cheeses.

33 rue des Moines 75017
+33 158591749
Closed Monday • €€€€

91 Marie-Anne Cantin

Recommended by Julie Neis

"One of the best cheese shops in Paris. Marie-Anne has various ages of Comté that are to die for. The shop is very small, but they'll help you pick out a selection of cheeses for your picnic, or vacuum-seal it for you to bring home on the plane in your luggage. Just tell them how big a slice you want" —*JN*

12 rue du Champ de Mars 75007
cantin.fr • +33 145504394
Open 7 days • €€€€

92 Quatrehomme

Recommended by Adrien, Joann Pai

Marie Quatrehomme is designated as a *Meilleur Ouvrier de France*, which means she is one of the best in France at her speciality. Quatrehomme has been going strong since 1953 with a reputation as one of the best cheese shops in the city. Marie is known in particular for her Beaufort and Saint-Marcellin, but you really can't go wrong in this tiny cheese wonderland.

62 rue de Sèvres 75007
(see website for other locations)
quatrehomme.fr • +33 147343345
Closed Sunday and Monday • €€€€

CHOCOLATE

Chocolate lovers, rejoice! For there will be no shortage of good chocolate to feast upon in Paris. When you go to a *chocolaterie*, you will know that you are in a place that really takes chocolate seriously – the best shops give you the feeling that you are walking into a jewellery store with all the precious jewels on display. The best approach is to ask for a *sachet* (little plastic bag), so that you can get a mixture of the chocolates they have sitting in the case. This is a great way to get to try a variety, and they will just weigh the bag at the end.

Most places will have chocolate bars (*tablettes*) in pretty wrappers that make great gifts. Some shops produce single-origin chocolate bars made with beans that come from a specific country, others specialise in unique fillings and ingredients, and nearly all of them have an option to purchase beautiful boxes so that you can transport them home in style. Some chocolate makers even craft chocolate into beautiful creations like high-heeled shoes, alligators or purses – *chocolatier* Patrick Roger (opposite) is known for making huge chocolate statues for his window displays (a recent example being a giant chocolate gorilla).

Each store is unique in its own way. Some have special creations that they're specifically known for, or a variety of chocolate pastries, or chocolates with a similar look but an array of unique fillings. They take their craft seriously and you can see it in the artistry of each little piece, while smelling the freshly made chocolate in the air.

See also La Grande Épicerie de Paris (page 102)

93 Patrick Roger

Recommended by Adrien, Raphaële Marchal, Julie Neis

"Patrick Roger is a must. I love to buy his famous praline chocolate bar as a snack – I can put my trainers on and go out just for that!" —*A*

"You can't go wrong here, it feels like shopping in a high-end jewellery store and he usually has some kind of enormous statue made of chocolate in the window. You can get a small bag with a mix of chocolates from the counter, or buy some bars to take home as gifts" —*JN*

4 place Saint-Sulpice 75006
patrickroger.com • +33 143298825
Closed Sunday • €€€€

94 Jean-Paul Hévin

Recommended by Raphaële Marchal, Lindsey Tramuta

Jean-Paul Hévin is regarded as one of the best *chocolatiers* in Paris. He makes an incredible variety of high-end chocolates, flavoured with all types of fillings including spices, caramels, pralines, fruit and ganache. These can make a great gift to bring home or just to indulge in yourself. You can also find chocolate pastries, chocolate éclairs, chocolate mousse and chocolate macarons.

231 rue Saint-Honoré 75001
(see website for other locations)
jeanpaulhevin.com • +33 155353596
Closed Sunday • €€€€

95 Edwart Chocolatier

Recommended by Natalia Esteves

"Co-founder Edwin Yansane is such a gentleman and a brilliant guy. Everything he does, he does with passion, and his chocolates are amazing"—*NE*

17 rue Vieille du Temple 75004
(see website for other locations)
edwart.fr • +33 142784892
Open 7 days • €€€€

96 À l'Étoile d'Or

Recommended by Maeve Schauerman Decouvelaere

"A quaint and cosy shop stocked full of France's best chocolates, sweets and cakes. The owner, Denise Acabo, is an absolute doll and will always be seen dressed in her signature kilt, necktie and pigtails"—*MSD*

30 rue Pierre Fontaine 75009
+33 148745955
Closed Sunday • €€€€

97 Jacques Genin

Recommended by Raphaële Marchal, Julie Neis, Lindsey Tramuta

"Jacques Genin is the master. I could kill for a slice of his flan. Go there for tea and cake, or to buy chocolates (*pralinés* there are mind-blowing), caramels (try the mango-passion fruit) or *pâtes de fruits* (lychee is my favourite)"—RM

"Jacques Genin provides chocolates for most of the 3-Michelin-starred restaurants in Paris, and he has a wide selection of unique flavours. Whatever you do, do not miss his caramels. Heaven"—JN

133 rue de Turenne 75003
(see website for other locations)
jacquesgenin.fr • +33 145772901
Closed Monday • €€€€

98 La Chocolaterie Cyril Lignac

Recommended by Joann Pai

"Great quality chocolates and I love the design"—*JP*

Cyril Lignac is a well-known pastry chef in Paris and he often hosts popular French TV culinary shows. His shops echo tradition and refinement, and his elegant pastries and chocolates are made with prestige ingredients. The creations depend on the creativity of the chefs and the seasons, but one of the most popular is the Equinoxe, a light chocolate ganache flavoured with Bourbon vanilla, a salted butter caramel filling and Speculoos biscuits.

25 rue Chanzy 75011
(see website for other locations)
lachocolateriecyrillignac.com
+33 155872140
Open 7 days • €€€€

MACARONS

Iconic, photogenic and impossibly delicate, there is much pleasure to be found in the perusing, purchasing and eating of Parisian macarons. The very best marry perfectly with their fillings – the first taste of a rose macaron really evokes the exact floral scent, and when you bite into a vanilla macaron, the purity of that vanilla bean envelops you such as to make you float, ever so slightly, above the ground. And the salted butter caramels? Always go for at least one of those, because everyone does theirs differently, and they are unspeakably good.

It's best to get a selection comprising, at the very least, a vanilla, a chocolate, a caramel, a fruit-flavoured and a floral. The two most popular macaron shops in Paris are without doubt Ladurée (page 126) and Pierre Hermé (page 128). Ladurée is on the more traditional side (credited with being the first tea salon in the world), whereas Pierre Hermé is more cutting-edge, experimenting with fun flavours and combinations. The only way to know which team you're on is to try both.

It's definitely worth seeking out places that are known for their macarons and making a dedicated trip there. You'll see macarons at random bakeries around town, but it's best to hold out for the good stuff.

Insider's tip: If you want to bring some of these delicate (and terribly crushable) beauties back with you, you can buy Ladurée macarons at the airport.

See also Jean-Paul Hévin (page 120)

99 Gérard Mulot

Recommended by Julie Neis

"Many people claim that Gérard Mulot makes their favourite macaron in the city. Though some of the colours can be a bit brighter (I tend to avoid neon macarons as a rule), these taste very fresh and natural. The textures of the shell and ratio of filling are spot on. He also makes an excellent *pain au chocolat* and delicious fruit tarts. You can even sign up for a tour of their flagship bakery"—*JN*

76 rue de Seine 75006
(see website for other locations)
maison-mulot.com • +33 143268577
Open 7 days • €€€€

100 Sadaharu Aoki

Recommended by Joann Pai

"This French-Japanese pastry shop has some of the best macarons in the city (and trust me, I've tried my fair share). Try the Asian-inspired flavours like black sesame and *genmaicha* (brown rice green tea)"—*JP*

35 rue de Vaugirard 75006
(see website for other locations)
sadaharuaoki.com • +33 145444890
Closed Monday • €€€€

101 Ladurée

Recommended by Julie Neis

"One of the most famous macaron boutiques in Paris. It was the first tea salon in the city and is credited as the inventor of the macaron. My favourite flavours are vanilla, dark chocolate, salted caramel and rose"—*JN*

75 avenue des Champs-Élysées 75008 (see website for other locations)
laduree.fr • +33 140750875
Open 7 days • €€€€

⓾ Pierre Hermé

Recommended by Adrien, Natalia Esteves, Julie Neis, Joann Pai, Maeve Schauerman Decouvelaere

"You can never go wrong with Pierre Hermé, especially his signature Mogador flavour (milk chocolate and passion fruit). It's a sincerely addictive experience! The vanilla and olive oil is a must too. My advice is to go for the mini ones so you can taste more flavours"—*A*

"A deliciously decadent treat, Pierre Hermé's macarons are that perfect soft, crunchy, melt-in-your-mouth texture. They are truly unbeatable"—*MSD*

4 rue Cambon 75001
(see website for other locations)
pierreherme.com • +33 143544777
Open 7 days • €€€€

RECIPES

Croque Monsieur

Steak Tartare

Sole Meunière

Crêpes with Nutella

Simple Millefeuille

The Perfect Picnic

The Ideal Cheese Board

Chocolat Chaud

Sidecar

Serendipiti

French 75

Croque Monsieur

An indulgent and comforting staple found in all Parisian cafés. Serve with lightly dressed rocket for a perfect solo lunch. You can freeze the leftover béchamel in portions, ready for the next time a croque craving hits.

Serves 1

2 medium slices of white bread

1 tsp grain mustard

2 thick slices of ham

3 tbsp cooled béchamel sauce (see below)

30g (a matchbox-sized piece) Gruyère, grated

For the béchamel

25g butter

25g plain flour

250ml milk

Pinch of freshly grated nutmeg

60g Gruyère, grated

Sea salt and freshly ground black pepper

Preheat the oven to 220°C.

To make the béchamel, heat the butter in a small pan over a medium-high heat. Once the butter is melted and frothing, add the flour and cook out, stirring constantly, for about a minute. Add the milk in thirds, whisking vigorously to prevent lumps. Once all the milk is incorporated, add the nutmeg and keep stirring until the mixture has thickened and will generously coat the back of a spoon. Take the pan off the heat, stir in the Gruyère, season to taste and set aside to cool slightly.

To assemble the croque monsieur, start by spreading the mustard evenly over one slice of bread. Cover the bread with the ham, then spread over 2 tablespoons of béchamel. Top with the other slice of bread and spread over the remaining tablespoon of béchamel. Sprinkle over the grated Gruyère and bake for 10–15 minutes, until brown and bubbling.

Steak Tartare

A bistro classic that's incredibly simple to make. Be sure to use the freshest steak and eggs you can lay your hands on.

Serves 2

350g beef fillet, well chilled

Handful of fresh parsley, finely chopped

1 large or 2 small shallots, finely chopped

1 tbsp capers, finely chopped

4 cornichons, finely chopped

1 tsp Dijon mustard

Dash of Tabasco sauce

2 egg yolks

Sea salt and freshly ground black pepper

Use a sharp knife to very finely chop the beef (having it as cold as possible will help).

Put the chopped meat into a bowl and lightly mix in all the other ingredients apart from the egg yolks. Taste and adjust the seasoning accordingly.

Spoon onto two plates, make an indentation in the top of each mound and top with an egg yolk. Serve immediately with *frites* or thin slices of toasted bread.

Sole Meunière

A lovely treatment for any white fish (just be sure to adjust the cooking time accordingly). Best served with boiled new potatoes and steamed seasonal greens.

Serves 2

2 fillets of sole, skin on (about 150g each)

3 tbsp plain flour, for dusting

1 tbsp vegetable oil

50g butter

Juice of ½ lemon

1 tbsp chopped fresh parsley or capers

Sea salt and freshly ground black pepper

Season both sides of the fish with salt and pepper before dipping into the flour and shaking off any excess.

Heat the oil in a wide non-stick frying pan over a medium-high heat. Add the fish fillets and cook, skin-side down for 2 minutes. Gently flip the fillets over and cook for 1 minute more.

Transfer to a warmed plate before putting the pan back on the heat and adding the butter. Allow the butter to bubble and froth and, when it has taken on a golden-brown colour, stir in the lemon juice and parsley or capers. Return the fish fillets to the pan and spoon the sauce over them. Serve immediately.

Crêpes with Nutella

A classic street food snack easily replicated at home. The evocative buttery smell will transport you straight back to the city of lights.

Serves 2 (makes about 6 pancakes)

100g plain flour

20g caster sugar

1 tsp baking powder

Pinch of salt

120ml milk

1 egg

50g butter, melted

Nutella, to serve

Combine the flour, sugar, baking powder and salt in a large bowl, then whisk in the remaining ingredients until you have a smooth batter.

Leave to rest for half an hour (if you can bear to wait).

Heat a non-stick frying pan over a medium heat. Once hot, ladle the batter into the pan and swirl to form a thin layer. Cook for 1–2 minutes, until the bottom is golden brown, then flip with a spatula and cook for another minute. Transfer to a warm plate and cover with foil and a tea towel while you make the rest.

Once ready, spread some Nutella (or any sweet topping of your choice) over each crêpe. Fold and enjoy.

Simple Millefeuille

The dessert of a thousand layers that excels in both flavour and texture. Often made with crème pâtissière, this simplified version uses Chantilly cream. Feel free to substitute the raspberries with any other soft fruit.

Serves 6

About 100g icing sugar, for rolling and dusting

250g puff pastry

200g raspberries

For the Chantilly cream

150ml whipping cream

50g icing sugar

½ tsp vanilla extract

Dust your work surface with plenty of icing sugar and roll out the puff pastry to a 30cm square, trimming the edges with a sharp knife. Cut the square into 3 equal strips, then cut each strip into 6 rectangles, giving you a total of 18 rectangles. Use a wide spatula to place on a baking tray lined with baking parchment and dusted with icing sugar. Chill in the fridge for at least 30 minutes.

When you're ready to bake, preheat the oven to 200°C. Dust the pastry rectangles heavily with icing sugar, then cover with a second sheet of baking parchment and another baking tray (this will prevent the pastry from puffing up too much while it cooks). Bake for 25 minutes, removing the second baking tray and layer of parchment halfway through.

To prepare the Chantilly cream, whip all the ingredients together until the mixture holds stiff peaks.

To assemble, dollop half of the Chantilly cream onto six of the cooled puff pastry rectangles, top with half of the raspberries and another pastry rectangle, then repeat. Top with the remaining pastry rectangles and give an extra dusting of icing sugar. Serve immediately.

The Perfect Picnic

With hundreds of scenic spots and delicious fresh produce to be found around almost every corner, Paris is a picnicker's delight (page 106).

The elements chosen are really up to you, but here are a few suggestions to get you started...

- **Baguette** Ask for *une baguette tradition* as they are made with dough that has been fermented for longer and are a step up in quality.
- **Roasted chicken** Found in markets throughout Paris – just follow your nose.
- **Charcuterie** *Jambon, saucisson, pâté, foie gras,* duck *rillettes*... There are so many options. Find a counter and point to whatever looks good.
- **Cheese** See page 112. Best to get as many as humanly possible. And maybe another baguette.
- **Veg** Avocado, tomato and pepper are probably enough. (This is a picnic, not a salad.)
- **Snacks** Olives, crisps, tapenade, cornichons and perhaps some fruit.
- **Wine** Rosé is a popular choice, but red, white and Champagne are equally refreshing.
- **Dessert** Either chocolates or some fancy dessert pastries from a pâtisserie. Or both.
- **Supplies** Corkscrew, picnic glasses, napkins and portable knife for cutting veggies and spreading cheese.

The Ideal Cheese Board

A well-considered cheese board can be a meal in itself and makes for a wonderful centrepiece that everyone can help themselves to and enjoy with plenty of wine. Preparing one can be lots of fun as there are so many options and any good cheese shop will let you try before you buy (see page 112).

Allow about 50g of cheese per person if you are serving as part of a meal, or 250g per person if it is the main event.

Try to include one of each of the following:
- Soft-ripened cow's cheese (such as Camembert or Brie)
- Soft-ripened goat's cheese (such as Chèvre, Cabichou or Sainte-Maure)
- Hard cheese (such as Comté, Cantal, Beaufort or Gruyère)
- Washed-rind cheese (such as Époisses, Reblochon or Maroilles)
- Blue cheese (such as Roquefort or Bleu d'Auvergne)

Serve with:
- Baguette
- Nuts such as almonds, walnuts or pecans
- Fresh fruit such as grapes, thinly sliced pear or ripe figs
- Something sweet and sticky such as fig jam or honey

Cheese is best served at room temperature so be sure to remove from the fridge about half an hour before serving. As a rule, start with the milder cheeses and work your way up to the most pungent – that way your palette has the best chance of experiencing all the different flavours.

Wines that come from the same region as a particular cheese often make for a good pairing. Other classics include Pinot Noir with Brie, Sauvignon Blanc with acidic goat's cheese, Chardonnay with Gruyère, and Sauternes with Roquefort.

Chocolat Chaud

Thick, voluptuous and miles away from the powdered stuff, a little cup of Parisian hot chocolate is indulgence at its best.

Serves 2

250ml whole milk

2 tsp icing sugar

75g dark chocolate, finely chopped

Whipped cream, to serve

Heat the milk and icing sugar in a small pan until warm but not boiling. Whisk the chocolate into the milk until fully incorporated. Thicken the mixture to a velvety texture by simmering and whisking constantly for 2–3 minutes. Serve warm in small cups with a dollop of whipped cream.

Sidecar

Punchy, powerful and beautifully well balanced, this golden tipple is the perfect way to start – or end – the evening.

Serves 1

50ml Cognac

50ml orange liqueur such as Cointreau

25ml lemon juice

25ml simple syrup

A splash of lime juice

Shake all the ingredients together with plenty of ice then strain into a chilled martini glass.

Serendipiti

A jovial and fruity number that was first created at the Ritz in Paris.

Serves 1

50ml Calvados

50ml apple juice

Champagne to fill

A sprig of mint

Pour the Calvados and apple juice into a tumbler with plenty of ice. Fill to the brim with Champagne and decorate with the mint.

French 75

A refreshing gin-based cocktail with the perfect balance of sweet and sour that is incredibly easy to recreate at home.

Serves 1

50ml gin

15ml lemon juice

10ml simple syrup

Champagne to fill

A twist of lemon

Shake the gin, lemon juice and syrup with plenty of ice. Strain into a chilled Champagne flute, top up with Champagne and decorate with a twist of lemon.

INDEX **A TO Z**

INDEX **BY ARRONDISSEMENT**

BLOOMSBURY PUBLISHING
Bloomsbury Publishing Plc
50 Bedford Square, London WC1B 3DP

BLOOMSBURY, BLOOMSBURY PUBLISHING and the Diana logo
are trademarks of Bloomsbury Publishing Plc

First published in Great Britain 2018

A catalogue record for this book is available from the British Library

ISBN: 978-1-4088-9324-1

2 4 6 8 10 9 7 5 3 1

Series Editor: Lena Hall
Contributing Writer: Julie Neis
Cover Designer: Greg Heinimann
Designer: Julyan Bayes
Photographer: Joann Pai
Production Controller: Arlene Alexander

Printed and bound in China by RR Donnelley Asia Printing Solutions Ltd

Bloomsbury Publishing Plc makes every effort to ensure that the papers used in the manufacture
of our books are natural, recyclable products made from wood grown in well-managed forests.
Our manufacturing processes conform to the environmental regulations of the country of origin

To find out more about our authors and books visit
www.bloomsbury.com and sign up for our newsletters

BREAKFAST

1	Café Oberkampf	I5
2	Carette	A5
3	Holybelly	H4
4	Chez Casimir	G2
5	KB Coffee Roasters	F2

PÂTISSERIE

6	Fou de Pâtisserie	G5
7	Bontemps	H5
8	La Pâtisserie des Rêves	D6
9	La Petite Rose	C2
10	Blé Sucré	J7

CRÊPES & GALETTES

11	Brutus	D2
12	La Crêperie de Josselin	D8
13	Breizh Café	H5

CLASSIC FRENCH

14	Au Pied de Cochon	F5
15	Les Deux Magots	E6
16	Les Arlots	G2
17	Astier	I4
18	Josephine Chez Dumonet	D8
19	Juste le Zinc	D2
20	Bistrot Paul Bert	J7
21	Chez La Vieille	F5

STEAK

22	Atelier Vivanda	E7
23	Les Parigots	H4
24	La Bourse et La Vie	F4
25	Clover Grill	F5
26	Brutos	J5
27	Le Relais de l'Entrecôte	B4

MODERN FRENCH

28	Ellsworth	F5
29	52 Faubourg Saint-Denis	G3
30	Dersou	I7
31	Septime	J6
32	Le Servan	J5
33	Tannat	I4

STREET FOOD

34	L'As du Fallafel	H6
35	Miznon	H6
36	Urfa Dürüm	G3
37	Berges de Seine	C5

SPECIAL OCCASION

38	L'Arpège	D6
39	L'Ami Jean	B5
40	Le Gabriel	C4
41	Le Clarence	C4
42	Verjus	F4

DESSERT & ICE CREAM

43	Berthillon	H7
44	Frenchie Bar à Vins	G4
45	Il Gelato del Marchese	F7
46	Une Glace à Paris	H6
47	Mokonuts	J7

SMALL PLATES & WINE

48	Le Grand Bain	J4
49	116 Pages	B4
50	Lucien La Chance	D1
51	La Cave à Michel	I3
52	La Buvette	J5
53	Compagnie des Vins	F7

APÉRO

54	La Palette	F6
55	La Fontaine de Belleville	I3
56	Pratz	E2
57	La Cave du Paul Bert	J7
58	Le Baron Rouge	J7
59	Septime la Cave	J6

COCKTAILS

60	La Commune	J4
61	Grand Pigalle	F2
62	Le Mary Celeste	H5
63	Lulu White	F2
64	Le Syndicat	G4

HOT DRINKS

65	Ten Belles	H3
66	Télescope	E4
67	The Broken Arm	H5
68	Lily of the Valley	H5
69	Boot Café	H5
70	Fragments	I6
71	Coutume Café	D7
72	Angelina	E5
73	Café de Flore	E6
74	Dose Dealer de Café	D1
75	La Mosquée Salon de Thé	G8

MARKETS

76	Marché des Enfants Rouges	H5
77	La Grande Épicerie de Paris	D7
78	Marché d'Aligre	J7
79	Marché Couvert Batignolles	D1
80	Marché Président Wilson	B5
81	Marché Bastille	I6

PICNICS

82	Lenôtre	I6
83	Cooperative Latte	G3
84	Kili Kio	H4
85	La Maison Plisson	I5
86	Causses	E2

CHEESE

87	Fromagerie Goncourt	I4
88	Taka & Vermo	G3
89	Le Bel Ordinaire	G3
90	Les Fromages des Batignolles	D1
91	Marie-Anne Cantin	B6
92	Quatrehomme	D7

CHOCOLATE

93	Patrick Roger	E7
94	Jean-Paul Hévin	E4
95	Edwart Chocolatier	H6
96	À l'Étoile d'Or	E2
97	Jacques Genin	H5
98	La Chocolaterie Cyril Lignac	J7

MACARONS

99	Gérard Mulot	F7
100	Sadaharu Aoki	E7
101	Ladurée	B4
102	Pierre Hermé	D4